The Samaritan Woman
RECONSIDERED

Eli Lizorkin-Eyzenberg, Ph.D.

JEWISH STUDIES
FOR CHRISTIANS

ISBN: 9781713300366

Table of Contents

To the Samaritan Woman who heard
the soft sound of sandaled feet.

To my friend Marjorie Murray
who also heard the same sound.

"Our vision is often
more abstracted by what
we think we know
than by our lack of
knowledge".

Krister Stendahl

Introduction

This book is a product of a prolonged personal study of the Gospel of John. A significant part of what I share here in "The Samaritan Woman Reconsidered" was already included in my "The Jewish Gospel of John: Discovering Jesus the King of All Israel" book. While the latter book is a detailed commentary on the entire Gospel of John this book is dedicated to the Samaritan Woman in particular. I decided to supply this rich Gospel story with additional context commentary which was not included in my longer book and focus exclusively on the fascinating conversation at the well.

This fourth chapter of John's Gospel, that relates the story of Jesus meeting the Samaritan woman at Jacob's well, begins by setting the stage for what will take place later in Samaria, and is rooted in what has already, by this time in the Gospel's progress, taken place in Judea. Jesus' rapidly growing popularity resulted in a significant following. Jesus' disciples performed an ancient Jewish ritual of ceremonial washing with water (known to us today as "baptism"), just as John the Baptist and his disciples did. The ritual represented people's confession of sin and their recognition of the need for the cleansing power of God's forgiveness. When it became clear to Jesus that the crowds were growing large, and especially when he heard that this alarmed the Pharisees, he decided it was time to go to Galilee through Samaria (verses 1-3). And this is where the story explained it this book occurred.

The Samaritan Woman is generally portrayed in our Bible studies as a woman of ill-repute. While avoiding people because of her deep shame over her immoral life, she seemingly stumbled upon Jesus resting at a well. However, most people reading this story are left with a nagging question. How could this woman receive an overwhelmingly positive response from her village neighbors, when she called them to drop everything and come with her to meet a Jewish man, she herself had just met? Something does not add up.

Come with me, reread this story, and let me share with you what I think really happened.

Dr. Eli Lizorkin-Eyzenberg

Samaria and Samaritans

Samaritan lands were sandwiched between Judea and Galilee, though not exclusively. They were situated within the borders of the land allotted to the sons of Joseph, Ephraim, and Menashe. (Today most Samaria and large parts of Judea constitute the disputed/occupied territories located in the Palestinian Authority).

Given Judeo-Samaritan tensions, which are similar in many ways to today's Israeli-Palestinian conflict, both groups tried to avoid passing through each other's territories when traveling. The way around Samaria for Judeans traveling to Galilee took twice as long as the three-day-direct journey from Galilee to Jerusalem, since avoiding Samaria required crossing the river Jordan twice to follow a path running east of the river (Josephus, Life 269). The way through Samaria was more dangerous because Samaritan-Jewish passions often ran high (Josephus, Antiquities. 20.118 and War 2.232). We are not told the reason Jesus and his disciples needed to go through Samaria. John simply says that Jesus "had to go"[1], implying that, for Jesus, just as it was for all other Jews, this was unusual.

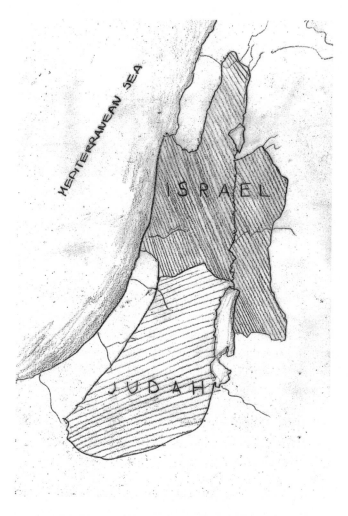

It is, of course, possible that Jesus needed to reach
Galilee relatively quickly. But the text gives us no

---

[1] The word "it is necessary" (δεῖ) occurs 10x in John (3:7, 14, 30; 4:4, 20, 24;
9:4; 10:16; 12:34; 20:9). Cf. the use of δεῖ in Luke-Acts.

indication that he had a pending invitation to an event in Galilee for which he was running late. The text only states that he left when he felt an imminent confrontation with the Pharisees over his popularity among Israelites was unavoidable. This was coupled with Jesus' understanding that the time for such a confrontation had not yet come.

In the mind of Jesus, the confrontation with the religious powerbrokers of Judea at this time was premature, and more needed to be done before going to the Cross and drinking the cup of God's wrath on behalf of his people. The way Jesus viewed Samaritans and his own ministry among them may surprise us as we continue looking into this story.

Jesus' journey through hostile and heretical territory has a meaning beyond any surface explanation. In a very real sense, God's unfathomable plan and mission, from the time His royal Son was eternally conceived in His mind, was to bind all of his beloved creation in redemptive unity. Jesus was sent to make peace between God and man, as well as between man and man. The accomplishment of this grand purpose began with the mission to unify Samaritan Israelites with the Israelites of Judea.

I know that this terminology is a little bit unusual, but I will continue to refer to Samaritans as Samaritan Israelites and to Jews as Judean Israelites because I believe both are Israelites. Though their ways have parted a long time ago, their ancient heritage is inseparable. Jesus' movements and activities were all done in accordance with his Father's will and leading. He only did what he saw the Father do (Jn. 5:19). This being the case, we can be certain that Jesus' journey through Samaria at this time was directed by his Father, and so too, was his conversation with the Samaritan woman.

First, the Samaritan Israelites defined their own existence in exclusively Israelite terms. The Samaritans called themselves – "the sons of Israel" and "the keepers" - *Shomrim*. Jewish sources refer to the Samaritans as *Kutim*. The term is most likely related to a location in Iraq from which the non-Israelite exiles were imported into Samaria (2 Kings 17:24). The name *Kutim* or *Kutites* was used in contrast to the term *Shomrim* which means the "keepers" – the terms that they reserved for themselves. Keepers of what? The old ways, ancient faith, tradition, covenant promises, of course. Jewish Israelite writings emphasized the foreign identity of Samaritan religion and practice in contrast to the true faith of Israel. The Samaritan Israelites believed that such identification denied their historical right of belonging to the people of Israel. The Samaritan Israelites were the faithful remnant of the Northern tribes – the keepers of the ancient faith.

Second, Samaritan Israelites had always opposed the worship of Israel's God in Jerusalem, believing instead that the center of Israel's worship was associated with Mt. Gerizim – the mount of YHWH's covenantal blessing (Deut. 27:12). On the other hand, Jewish/Judean Israelites believed Mt. Zion in Jerusalem was the epicenter of spiritual activity in

Israel. One of the reasons for the rejection of the prophetic Jewish writings by the Samaritan Israelites was that the Hebrew prophets supported Jerusalem and the Davidic dynasty.

Third, the Samaritans had a fourfold creed: 1) One God – YHWH, 2) One Prophet – Moses, 3) One Book – Torah, and 4) One place – Mt. Gerizim. Most Jewish Israelites of Jesus' day agreed with the Samaritan Israelites on two of these points: "one God" and "one Book". They disagreed on the identity of the place of worship and on other books that should also have been accepted by the people of Israel – the Prophets and the Writings.

Fourth, the Samaritans believed the Judean Israelites had taken the wrong path in their religious practice of the ancient Israelite faith, which they branded as heretical, as the Jews did of the Samaritan's faith expression. The relationship between these two ancient groups can be compared to the sharp disagreements between Shia and Sunni Muslims today. To outsiders, both groups are Muslim, but not to the Shia and the Sunni. To them – one is true and the other is false; one is real and the other is an imposter. The Samaritan – Jewish conflict was in this sense very similar. In many ways, this conflict defined the inner Israelite polemic of the first century.

Fifth, as was mentioned before, the Samaritans are not to be confused with a syncretistic people group that also lived in Samaria (gentile residents of Samaria), who were most probably the people who approached returnees to Jerusalem to help them build the Jerusalem Temple and were rejected by them (Ezra 4:1-2). When Assyrians conquered the Northern Kingdom of Israel they repopulated the desolate lands with subjects from their own kingdom, loyal to the throne. And these transplants from Mesopotamia lived alongside impoverished and devastated local population, the remnant of those who were not led away into slavery. Due to the theology and rejection of the Davidic dynasty, by the Northern tribes the Samaritan Israelites, the remnant of devastated kingdom of Israel, could not support Temple building in Jerusalem. In 2 Chronicles 30:1-31:6 we are told that not all the people from the northern kingdom of Israel were exiled by the Assyrians. Most of them remained even after the Assyrian conquest of the land in the 8th century BCE, preserving ancient Israelite traditions that would differ from later innovations of the Judean version of Israel's faith.

It is quite likely that some segments of the local population mixed with the transplants from the Assyrian empire. So as a result, three kinds of people populated Samaria: the descendants of the Northern Tribes of Israel who kept the old ways, the foreigners transplanted from Assyrian lands, and a newly-blended combination of the two. The confusing part is that all of them, regardless of their actual heritage or ideology, were called "Samaritans" because they lived in Samaria. So how can one know which Samaritan one encounters in the story? This is not easy, but the answer is - the context should give us a clue. This is why it is important to highlight the descendants of the Northern Tribes of Israel as Samaritan Israelites.

Sixth, the Samaritan Israelites used what is now called "Samaritan Hebrew" in a script that is the direct descendent of Paleo-Hebrew (ancient Hebrew), while the Jewish Israelites adopted a new form of square, stylized letters that were part of the Aramaic alphabet. Moreover, by the time of Jesus, the Samaritan Israelites were also heavily Hellenized in Samaria proper and in the diaspora. Just as the Jewish Israelites had the Septuagint, the Samaritan Israelites had their own translation of the Torah into Greek, called *Samaritikon.*

And lastly, the Samaritan Israelites believed that their version of the Torah was the original version and the Jewish Torah was the edited version, which had been changed by Babylonian Jews. Conversely, the Judeans charged that the Samaritan Torah represented an

.

edition edited to reflect the views of the Samaritans. As you can see, this was not an easy relationship.

But you may be familiar that the authors of the New Testament express favorable attitudes towards Samaritans. Who has not heard the parable of the Good Samaritan (Lk 10:25-37)? For centuries, Jesus' tale has inspired people to help their neighbors. What made the good Samaritan so good to the first-century Jewish audience? Why did Jesus even tell this story? There are parts of this story that people often miss only because they are unfamiliar with first-century Judaism. One reason may be that he saw what he thought was a dead body on the side of the road and did not ignore it. What many readers of the story fail to consider that the Samaritan and others who passed by did not know the person was alive. Once the Samaritan tried to help the stranger he realized that he was alive.

In Jewish culture to be unburied was perceived as a curse. Elijah prophesied that Jezebel would meet this ugly fate and, indeed, her dead body was torn apart by wild dogs (2 Kgs 9:34-35). In Babylonian exile, a righteous man named Tobit secretly buried the bodies of other Jews whom the king had slaughtered (Tobit 1: 16-20; c. 2nd century BCE). Mishnah preserves rabbinic thinking on the matter

> "A High Priest and a nazir [a person who took a Nazarite vow] may not become impure for their relatives (Lev 21:11), but

may for an abandoned dead body." (m.
Nazir 7:1).

Many people do not know this, but for ancient rabbis,
even priestly purity was secondary to deeds of
kindness. Indeed, the Torah associates dead things
with ritual impurity, and Moses did not give any
commands obligating one to bury an abandoned body.
Those who passed the supposed corpse on the side of
the road could have shown mercy, but instead, they
followed the letter of the law. The poor guy was dead.

In Jesus' day burying a body that no one else could
care for was seen as a highly ethical deed, as a selfless
act of kindness that cannot be repaid. Jesus asked,
*"Which… proved to be a neighbor…" and he was told, "the
one who showed mercy toward him" (Lk 10:36-37)*. The
answer is obvious, the Samaritan, the person many
would not expect to go beyond the norm is the one
who showed extraordinary kindness to someone who
was not literally his neighbor.

In Jesus' teaching *helios* "compassion" "mercy" or
"loving-kindness" *chesed* towards other people
transcends all other commandments. A Samaritan was
an outsider, with no obligation to care for the corpse
of a Jew, yet he showed compassion and thereby acted
as a good neighbor. Let's keep such positive Jewish
perspectives on Samaritans in balance with the ill
feelings of a long dispute about who is right. Its time
to look at the woman by the well.

MY REQUEST

Dear reader, may I ask you for a favor? Would you take three minutes of your time and provide an encouraging feedback to other people shopping on Amazon.com about this book (assuming you like it of course!)?

Here is how: 1. Go to Amazon.com and search for the title of this book – "The Samaritan Woman Reconsidered". 2. Click on the title, click on the "ratings" link (right under the author's name) and click "Write a customer review" button. 3. Rate the book and leave a few words.

This will really help me a lot, especially if you genuinely love this book! After writing a review please drop me a personal note and let me know - dr.eli.israel@gmail.com. I would appreciate your help with this.

Dr. Eli Lizorkin-Eyzenberg

The Encounter at the Well

In describing the encounter, John makes several interesting observations that have major implications for our understanding of verses 5-6: *"So he came to a town in Samaria called Sychar, near the plot of ground Jacob had given to his son Joseph. Jacob's well was there, and Jesus, tired as he was from the journey, sat down by the well. It was about the sixth hour."* John mentions the Samaritan town named Sychar. It is not clear if Sychar was a village very near Shechem or if Shechem itself is in view. The text simply calls our attention to a location near the plot of ground Jacob gave to his son Joseph. Whether or not it was the same place, it was certainly in the same vicinity, at the foot of Mt. Gerizim.

While this is interesting and it shows that John was indeed a local, knowing the detailed geography of the place, it is no less important, and perhaps even more significant, that the Gospel's author calls the reader's attention to the presence of a silent witness to this encounter: the bones of Joseph.[2] This is how the book of Joshua relates to that event:

---

[2] Josh. 24:32; Josephus, Ant. 2.8.2.

"Now they buried the bones of Joseph, which the sons of Israel brought up from Egypt, at Shechem, in the piece of ground which Jacob had bought from the sons of Hamor the father of Shechem for one hundred pieces of money; and they became the inheritance of Joseph's sons" (Josh. 24:32).

The reason for this reference to Joseph in verse 5 will only become clear when we see that the Samaritan woman suffered in a manner similar to Joseph. If this reading of the story is correct, just as Joseph endured unexplained suffering for the purpose of bringing salvation to Israel; likewise the Samaritan woman endured suffering which led to the salvation of the Samaritan Israelites in that locale (4:39-41).

> *"⁶Jacob's well was there, and Jesus, tired as he was from the journey, sat down by the well. It was about the sixth hour".*

It has traditionally been assumed that the Samaritan woman was a woman of ill repute. The reference to the sixth hour (about midday) has been interpreted to mean that she was avoiding the water drawing crowd of other women in the town. The biblical sixth hour[3] was supposedly the worst possible time of the day to leave one's dwelling and venture out into the scorching heat. "If anyone were to come to draw water at this hour, we could appropriately conclude that they were trying to avoid people", the argument goes. We are, however, suggesting another possibility.

The popular theory views her as a particularly sinful woman who had fallen into sexual sin and therefore was called to account by Jesus about the multiplicity of husbands in her life. Why did she have so many husbands? Jesus told her, as the popular theory has it, that He knew that she had five previous husbands and that she was living with her current "boyfriend" outside the bonds of marriage, and therefore she was in no condition to play spiritual games with Him! In this view, the reason she avoided the crowd was precisely because of her reputation for short-lived marital commitments. But there are problems with this theory.

First, midday is not the worst time to be out in the sun. If it was 3 pm (ninth hour) the traditional theory would make better sense. Moreover, it is not at all

---

[3] Hence the shock of the darkness at the sixth hour when Jesus died (Matt. 27:45; Mk. 15:33; Lk. 23:44).

clear that this took place during the summer months, which could make the weather in Samaria altogether irrelevant. Secondly, is it possible that we are making too much of her going to draw water at "an unusual time?" Don't we all sometimes do regular things during unusual hours and could it be possible that this is such a case? This does not necessarily mean we are hiding something from someone. For example, we read that Rachel came to the well with her sheep probably also at about the same time (Gen. 29:6-9).

There are also other problems with this reading of the text. When we try to understand this story with the traditional mindset, we can't help but wonder how it was possible, in this conservative Samaritan Israelite society, that a woman with such a bad track record of supporting community values could have caused the entire village to drop everything and go with her to see Jesus (4:30). The standard logic is as follows: She had led such a godless life that when others heard of her excitement and newfound spiritual interest, they responded in awe and went to see Jesus for themselves. This rendering, while possible, seems unlikely to the author of this book, and seems to read much later theological (evangelical) approaches into this ancient story, which had its own historical setting. I am persuaded that reading the story in a new way is more logical and creates less interpretive problems than the commonly held view.

Let us take a closer look at John 4:7-9:

> *"When a Samaritan woman came to draw water, Jesus said to her, 'Will you give me a drink?' (His disciples had gone into the town to buy food). The Samaritan woman said to him, 'You are a Jew and I am a Samaritan woman. How can you ask me for a drink?' (For "the Jews" do not associate with Samaritans)".*

In spite of the fact that, to the modern eye, the differences were insignificant and unimportant, Jesus and the nameless Samaritan woman were from two different and historically adversarial people, each of whom considered the other to have deviated drastically from the ancient faith of Israel. As mentioned above, a modern parallel to the Judeo-Samaritan conflict would be the sharp animosity between Shia and Sunni Muslims. For most of us today Muslims are Muslims, but within Islam, this is not an agreed-upon proposition. Both parties consider each other as the greatest enemy of true Islam. So, too, for the people in the ancient world. These two warring people groups were Israelites and were both a part of the same faith. However, they were bitter enemies. This was not because they were so different, but precisely because they were very much alike.

Both Israelite groups considered the other to be imposters. While we don't have Samaritan sources to tell us their official position, we do know that a later source, the Babylonian Talmud, referring to the views and practices of the distant past, states: "Daughters of the Samaritans are menstruants from the cradle"

(Babylonian Talmud, Niddah 31b) and therefore any item that they handled would be unclean to the Judean[4].

The Samaritan woman probably recognized that Jesus was Judean by his distinctive Jewish traditional clothing and his accent (It is highly likely that the conversation took place in the tongue  familiar to them both). Jesus would have most certainly worn ritual fringes (tzitzit) in obedience to the Torah/Law of Moses (Num. 15: 38 and Deut. 22:12), but since Samaritan Israelite men observed Torah as well, this would not have been a distinguishing factor. The difference between these two groups was not whether the Torah of Moses must be obeyed, but *how* it should be obeyed.

Gender relationships have changed throughout the ages of history, affected by culture and social boundaries. I

---

[4] The Mishnah also explores the ritual and ethnic identity of Samaritans (mDem. 3:4; 5:9; 6:1; 7:4; mShev. 8:10; mTer. 3:9; mSheqal. 1:5; mKetub. 3:1).

would suggest that we know little of what ancient Israelites felt about the proximity of genders and touch because we are profoundly affected by our own cultural ideas without evening realizing it. One text that remains an enigma to most Christ-followers is the post-resurrection story in the twentieth chapter of John's gospel where Jesus cautions Mary to avoid touching him, but a week later invites Thomas to do just that.

Mary, seeing her beloved and presumed-dead rabbi now alive, attempted to hug the resurrected Jesus (vs. 16). He emphatically told her that she could not touch him because He had not yet ascended to his Father (vs. 17). Shortly after (when all the disciples were gathered to regroup) Christ appeared to them resurrected! Thomas was absent from this gathering (vss. 19-21). Later, when the disciples reported to Thomas that they had seen Jesus alive, he understandably responded with skepticism (vs. 24). Eight days later, Jesus unexpectedly appeared again to the gathered disciples and challenged Thomas to touch him by placing his hands into the holes that remained in his body (vs. 26-27). The obvious question is this: why did Jesus deny Mary, but later encourage Thomas to touch Him?

In order to understand Jesus' very different instructions to Mary and Thomas, we need to understand the purity requirement for the Jewish High Priest on the Day of Atonement. The High Priest was forbidden to come into contact with anything that was ceremonially unclean in order to avoid being disqualified to enter God's presence the following day. So much depended on this ritual purity! After His resurrection, Jesus (as our ultimate High Priest) would shortly be ministering in the heavenly tabernacle (Heb. 9:11). It is significant that Jesus appeared to the disciples and told Thomas to touch him after eight days because it takes seven days to ordain a priest (Ex. 29:35).

The most likely reason for Jesus' instructions to Mary not to touch him had to do with the fact that He was determined to enter the heavenly tabernacle in a ready-to-serve, consecrated state. Defilement would not be a sin, but it would have disqualified Him (for a period of time) from entering God's presence. Mary may have had a number of reasons for defilement (possible menstrual circle, stepping into the tomb, etc), Jesus' priestly mission was too important to allow for any possibility of failure. By the time Jesus met Thomas, His priestly work is done. He had returned from completing His duties and possible defilement was no longer an issue. So it is not that a woman could not come close and touch Jesus because something was wrong with them touching or being close. At that moment her touch would interrupt something supremely important. The reason is veiled from most people because we fail to understand this sort of life. It is not a part of our modern world and thinking.

Jesus' role as a prophet was carried out during His earthly life. His role as king was yet to be realized at the time of the ascension. He first needed to be ordained a priest and carry out His duties in the heavenly tabernacle! Nothing could be permitted to stand in the way of his mission.

The same is with the Samaritan woman. You want to drink from my water vessel? You want to touch something of mine, she says to Jesus? That is her puzzled response. But does that response have more to do with her being a woman or a Samaritan? We often transfer our own ideas about gender proximity into ancient stories like this one. But we do not fully understand what reasons stand behind distance and proximity between people depicted in such ancient settings.

Relationships between people groups can be very controversial. Outsiders rarely understand what is the reason they dislike each other and why they can't get along. If outsiders ever hear some of the reasons they appear trivial. The apprehension of inter-ethnic contact is rarely appreciated by modern people living in ethnically diverse modern societies. By that was not the world of the gospels.

Two Gospels record a meeting between Judean Jesus and a Greek woman. (Mk.7:24-29; Matt.15:21-28). Jesus goes to Tyre and Sidon (allotment territory of the tribe of Asher that was never fully taken over by Israelite). There he meets a desperate mother willing to do anything for her suffering child: *"Have mercy on me, Lord, Son of David! My daughter is severely tormented by a demon"* (Mat. 15:21-22). As we continue reading we see that Jesus first gave her the silent treatment. Then, when his

Jewish disciples demanded he answer her, he responded: *"I was sent only to the lost sheep of the house of Israel".* However, the woman was relentless. *"She came, knelt before him, and said, "Lord, help me!" He answered her: "It isn't right to take the children's bread and throw it to the dogs"* (Mat. 15:23-26).

The most offensive statement, of course, has to do with Jesus' comparison of Greek Gentiles to dogs. The key to understanding this text is found in the realization that only in the modern Western world dogs are thought to be part of the family. Dogs (often) live inside and not outside of the family home, but it was not so in ancient times in the East. In other words, the comparison to dogs was not meant to dehumanize the Greek woman but to emphasize that Jesus' primary mission was to Israel – to those inside of God's family, not outside of it.

Understood this way, we see that there was nothing dehumanizing in Jesus' response. It is no different from what Apostle Paul would later write: *"…the power of God for salvation to everyone who believes, first to the Jew, and also to the Greek".* In spite of some misunderstood statements about his seeming disregard for the physical family, Jesus here says – family first! But what made Jesus act differently towards her now? Clearly it was her response: *"Yes, Lord", she said, "yet even the dogs eat the crumbs that fall from their masters' table". Then Jesus replied to her, "Woman, your faith is great. Let it be done for you as you want".* (Matthew 15:27-28)

This Sidonian woman displayed the true faith of Israel exemplified in the Torah by both Abraham and Moses. Just like them, she was willing to argue with God, believing with unwavering faith that He is just, good and merciful. This is not exactly the position of Samaritans. As far as they were concerned the Judeans were wrong and Samaritans followed the true way.

Jesus continues:

> *10 "If you knew the gift of God and who it is that asks you for a drink, you would have asked him and he would have given you living water.' 11 'Sir,' the woman said, 'you have nothing to draw with and the well is deep. Where can you get this living water? 12 Are you greater than our father Jacob, who gave us the well and drank from it himself, as did also his sons and his flocks and herds?"13 Jesus answered, 'Everyone who drinks this water will be thirsty again, 14 but whoever drinks the water I give him will never thirst. Indeed, the water I give him will become in him a spring of water welling up to eternal life'. 15 The woman said to him, 'Sir, give me this water so that I won't get thirsty and have to keep coming here to draw water'. 16 He told her, 'Go, call your husband and come back'. 17 'I have no husband,' she replied. Jesus said to her, 'You are right when you say you have no husband. 18 The fact is, you have had five husbands, and the man you now have is not your husband. What you have just said is*

> *quite true.'* [19] *'Sir,' the woman said, 'I can see that you are a prophet.* [20] *Our fathers worshiped on this mountain, but you "Jews" claim that the place where we must worship is in Jerusalem'".*

This passage has often been interpreted as follows: "Jesus initiates a spiritual conversation (vs. 10). The woman begins to ridicule Jesus' statement by pointing out his inability to provide what he seems to offer (verses 11-12). After a brief confrontation in which Jesus points out the lack of an eternal solution to the woman's spiritual problem (verses 13-14), the woman continues with a sarcastic attitude (vs. 15) Finally, Jesus has had enough and he then forcefully exposes the sin in the woman's life – a pattern of broken family relationships. (verses 16-18) Now, cut to the heart by Jesus' all-knowing x-ray vision, the woman acknowledges her sin in a moment of truth (vs. 19) by calling Jesus a prophet. But then, as every unbeliever usually does, she tries to avoid the real issues of her sin and her spiritual need by raising doctrinal issues (vs. 20), in order to avoid dealing with the real issues in her life". Though this may not be the only way this text is commonly understood, it does follow a generally negative view of the Samaritan woman.

Because this popular interpretation presupposes that the woman was particularly immoral, it sees the entire conversation in light of that negative viewpoint. I would like to recommend a wholly different trajectory for understanding this story. Though it is not an airtight case, this alternative trajectory seems to be a

29

better fit for the rest of the story, and especially for its conclusion. At the very least, it deserves your attention and evaluation.

MY REQUEST

Dear reader, may I ask you for a favor? Would you take three minutes of your time and provide an encouraging feedback to other people shopping on Amazon.com about this book (assuming you like it of course!)?

Here is how: 1. Go to Amazon.com and search for the title of this book – "The Samaritan Woman Reconsidered". 2. Click on the title, click on the "ratings" link (right under the author's name) and click "Write a customer review" button. 3. Rate the book and leave a few words.

This will really help me a lot, especially if you genuinely love this book! After writing a review please drop me a personal note and let me know - dr.eli.israel@gmail.com. I would appreciate your help with this.

Dr. Eli Lizorkin-Eyzenberg

Rereading the Samaritan Woman Story

As was previously suggested, it is possible the Samaritan woman was not trying to avoid anyone. But, even if she was, there are explanations for her avoidance other than feeling guilty about her sexual immorality. For example, as you well know, people don't want to see anyone when they are depressed. Depression was present in Jesus' time, just as it is present in people's lives today. Instead of assuming that the Samaritan woman changed husbands like gloves, it is just as reasonable to think of her as a woman who had experienced the deaths of several husbands, or as a woman whose husbands may have been unfaithful to her, or even as a woman whose husbands divorced her for her inability to have children. In ancient Israelite society, women did not initiate divorces. Any of these mentioned suggestions and others are possible in this instance.

The book of Tobit (2nd century BCE), for example, speaks about a Jewish woman named Sarah who had seven husbands who, with the help of demonic forces, each died on the day of his wedding. She was scorned by the community, looked upon as cursed and guilty of their deaths. Depressed to the point of suicide, Sarah prayed to God to end her shame, insisting on her purity to the end (Tobit 3:7-17). People behaved harshly toward Sarah. No doubt the social standing of the Samaritan woman brought her great anguish as well. My own Great Aunt had four husbands and she outlived them all. So I know this happens.

Can you imagine the stigma this Samaritan woman might have experienced? Any man she marries ends up dead. Every marriage she enters falls apart. It would be so easy for some evil tongues in her village to suggest that she is cursed...

Jesus stated that she lived with a man who was not her husband. Many assume this meant the woman lived with her boyfriend, but that is not stated. Perhaps she needed help and lived with a distant relative, or in some other undesirable arrangement, in order to survive. Jesus was not nailing her to the cross of justice, but instead was letting her know that he knew everything about the pain she endured. This is certainly more in keeping with the Jesus we know from other instances in his life.

By the way, the overwhelming majority of Western art pictures the Samaritan Woman at the well as young, attractive, well dressed and adorned with some jewelry. Countless paintings that illustrate this biblical scene make her appear desirable in one or another way. Well, if we buy into the idea of her being a woman of loose moral she must look the part of a temptress. How else would she be able to lure all these men into her life? Out imagination is boundless. But that is only that – imagination coupled with popular culture images which fuel it. The Gospel of John does not reveal any such details.

If I was to guess, she was probably in her forties and probably not as good looking or fair-skinned as the woman on the cover of this book. She lived a difficult life and probably worked hard every day just to survive. The cover for this book is an intentional pun, a pop-culture caricature, a Hollywood version many people imagine. It is unlikely she looked this good. It is unlikely she was even trying to look attractive of presentable going to draw water from the well.

If I am correct in my suggestion that this woman was not a "fallen woman," then perhaps we can connect her amazingly successful testimony to the village with John's unexpected, but extremely important, reference to the bones of Joseph. It is worthy of note that for the Samaritan readership of this Gospel, the reference to the place of Joseph's bones and Jacob's well would be highly significant. When we understand that the conversation took place next to Joseph's bones, we are immediately reminded of Joseph's story and his *mostly* undeserved suffering. As you may remember, only part of Joseph's suffering was self-inflicted. Yet in the end, when no one saw it coming, the sufferings of Joseph turned into events leading from starvation and death to salvation.

Now let us consider the connection with Joseph in more detail. Shechem was one of the cities of refuge where a man who had killed someone unintentionally was provided a safe haven in Israel (Josh. 21:20-21)[5]. As inhabitants of Shechem were living out their lives in the shadow of the Torah's prescription, they were no doubt keenly aware of the unusual status of grace

---

[5] Cities of refuge: Num. 35:1-15; Shechem as city of refuge (Josh. 20; 1 Chr. 6:67).

and God's protective function that was allotted to their special city. They were to protect people who were unfortunate, whose lives were threatened by avenging family members, but who were not actually guilty of any *intentional* crime deserving the threatened punishment.

Joseph was born into a very special family, where grace and salvation should have been a characteristic description. Jacob, the descendant of Abraham and Isaac, had eleven other sons, whose actions, (apart from Benjamin) instead of helping their father raise Joseph, ranged from outbursts of jealousy to a desire to get rid of their spoiled but "special" brother forever. But there was more. It was in Shechem that Joshua assembled the tribes of Israel, challenging them to abandon their former gods in favor of YHWH and, after making a covenant with them, he buried Joseph's bones there. We read in Josh. 24:1-32:

> *"Then Joshua assembled all the tribes of Israel at Shechem.* He summoned the elders, leaders, judges and officials of Israel, and they presented themselves before God… But if serving the LORD seems undesirable to you, then choose for yourselves this day whom you will serve, whether the gods your forefathers served beyond the River or the gods of the Amorites, in whose land you are living. But as for me and my household, we will serve the LORD. …*On that day Joshua made a covenant for the people, and there at Shechem he drew up for them decrees*

and laws. And Joshua recorded these things in the Book of the Law of God. Then he took a large stone and set it up there under the oak near the holy place of the LORD… Israel served the LORD throughout the lifetime of Joshua and of the elders who outlived him and who had experienced everything the LORD had done for Israel. *And Joseph's bones, which the Israelites had brought up from Egypt, were buried at Shechem in the tract of land that Jacob bought for a hundred pieces of silver from the sons of Hamor, the father of Shechem. This became the inheritance of Joseph's descendants".*

It is interesting that the place for this encounter with the Samaritan woman was chosen by the Lord of providence in such a beautiful way: an emotionally alienated woman, who felt unsafe, ironically lived in or near a city of refuge and is having a faith-finding, covenant-renewing conversation with God's Royal Son, Jesus, who has come to reunite all Israel with her God. She does so at the very place where the ancient Israelites renewed their covenant in response to God's words, sealing them with two witnesses: 1) the stone (Josh. 24:26-27) – confessing with their mouths their covenant obligations and faith in Israel's God, and 2) the bones of Joseph (Josh. 24:31-32) – whose story guided them in their travels.

In a sense, the Samaritan woman does the same thing as the ancient Israelites – confessing her faith in Jesus as the Christ and covenant Savior of the world, to her fellow villagers, as we read in John 4:29-39:

> *"Come, see a man who told me everything. Could this be the Christ?" They came out of the town and made their way toward him... Many of the Samaritans from that town believed in him because of the woman's testimony..."*

The connection between Joseph and the Samaritan woman does not end there. We might recall that Joseph had received a special blessing from his father at the time of Jacob's death. It was a promise that he would be a fruitful vine climbing over a wall (Gen. 49:22). Psalm 80:8 speaks of a vine being brought out of Egypt, whose shoots spread throughout the earth, eventually bringing salvation to the world through the *true vine*. In John 15:1 we read that Jesus identified himself as this *true vine*.

Like Israel of old, Jesus was also symbolically brought out of Egypt (Matt. 2:15). In his conversation with the Samaritan woman, Jesus – the promised vine in Jacob's promise to Joseph – was in effect climbing over the wall of hostility between the Judean and Samaritan Israelites to unite these two parts of His Kingdom through His person, teaching and deeds. In a deeply symbolic fashion, this conversation takes place at the very well that was built by Jacob, to whom the promise was given!

Now that we have reviewed some of the relevant Hebrew Bible/Old Testament symbolism, let us now reread this story through a different lens. It may have gone something like this:

Jesus initiated a conversation with the woman: "Will you give me a drink?" His disciples had gone into town to buy food. The woman felt safe with Jesus because, not only is he not from her village, but he didn't know about her failed life or even how depressed she may have felt for months. In her view, he was part of a heretical, though related, religious community. Jesus would have had no contact with the Israelite Samaritan leaders of her community.

> *"If you knew the gift of God and who it is that asks you for a drink, you would have asked him and he would have given you living water", says Jesus.*

It is important that we picture the woman. She was not laughing; she was having an informed, deeply theological and spiritual discussion with Jesus. This was a daring attempt to ascertain the truth that was outside her accepted theological framework and surely would not pass the test of cultural sensibilities of "faithful" Samaritans. She took issue with Jesus, precisely because she took the word of God (Samaritan Torah) seriously:

> *"'Sir,' the woman said, 'you have nothing to draw with and the well is deep. Where can you get this living water? Are you greater than our*

father Jacob, who gave us the well and drank
from it himself, as did also his sons and his
flocks and herds?' Jesus answered: 'Everyone
who drinks this water will be thirsty again,
but whoever drinks the water I give him will
never thirst. Indeed, the water I give him will
become in him a spring of water welling up to
eternal life.' The woman said to him, 'Sir, give
me this water so that I won't get thirsty and
have to keep coming here to draw water'".

This theme of water[6] will be repeated many times in John's Gospel, but even at this point, we can see Jesus' and John's preoccupation with water as being related to Temple imagery. We will return to this theme in the coming chapters.

After the above interaction, which strikes a familiar chord for the Christian who has experienced the life-giving power of Jesus' presence and spiritual renewal, Jesus continued the conversation. He let the nameless Samaritan woman know that He understood her troubles much more fully than she thought. He did this by showing her that he was aware of the pain and suffering she had endured during her life.

> *"He told her, 'Go, call your husband and*
> *come back'. 'I have no husband,' she replied.*
> *Jesus said to her, 'You are right when you say*
> *you have no husband. The fact is, you have*
> *had five husbands, and the man you now have*

---

[6] Cf. John 1:26-33; 2:6-9; 3:5, 23; 4:7-28; 4:46; 5:7; 7:38; 13:5; 19:34.

is not your husband. What you have just said
is quite true'".

We must try and disconnect from the usual view of this passage and allow for another interpretive possibility. Do you recall the seemingly obscure reference to Joseph's bones, which was very meaningful to first century Israelites, being buried near this very place where the conversation took place? At the beginning of the story, John wanted us to remember Joseph. He was a man who suffered much in his life;[7] but whose suffering was ultimately used for the salvation of Israel and the known world. Under Joseph's leadership, Egypt became the only nation that acted wisely by saving grain during the years of plenty and then being able to feed others during the years of famine (Gen. 41:49-54).

It is highly symbolic that this conversation took place in the presence of a silent witness: the bones of Joseph. God first allowed terrible physical, psychological and social injustice to be done to Joseph; He then used this suffering to greatly bless those who came in contact with him. Instead of reading this story in terms of Jesus nailing the immoral woman to the cross of God's standard of morality, we should read it in terms of God's mercy and compassion for the broken world in general, and for marginalized Israelites (Samaritans) in particular.

---

[7] It is intriguing to think that, perhaps, there is also some connection to the rape of Dinah and the further violence that followed as a result (Gen.34) since these events too are associated with this location.

According to the popular view, it is at this point, convicted by Jesus' prophetic rebuke, that the woman seeks to change the subject and avoid the personal nature of the encounter by engaging in unimportant theological controversy. The problem is, although these matters may be unimportant to the modern reader, they were of very real concern to the ancient readers, especially those who lived with the Judean-Samaritan conflict. Therefore, let us consider an alternative interpretation.

Having seen Jesus' intimate knowledge of her miserable situation and his compassionate empathy, the woman felt secure enough to also break tradition and climb over the wall of forbidden associations. She makes a statement that invites Jesus' commentary on the subject of the key theological difference between the Judeans and the Samaritans.

> *"'Sir,' the woman said, 'I can see that you are a prophet. Our fathers worshiped on this mountain, but you 'Jews' claim that the place where we must worship is in Jerusalem'".*

The Samaritans were Mt. Gerizim-centered Israelites in their understanding of the Pentateuch (Torah), while the Jews were Mt. Zion-centered[8] in their interpretation of essentially the same body of literature, admittedly with occasional variations. This question seems trivial to a modern Christian who

---

[8] Mt. Zion as epicenter (Ps. 2:6; 9:11, 14; 14:7; 20:2; 48:2; 48:11-12; 50:2; etc.; 1QM 12:13; 19:5).

usually thinks what is really important is that one can confess: "Jesus is in *my* life as a *personal* Lord and Savior". But, while the Samaritan woman's question may not concern us today, it was a major issue in the first century. Indeed, this deeply theological and spiritual conversation was a very important intersection on the road of human history, because of the tremendous impact it has had on the entire world, ever since this encounter took place.

With fear and trepidation, the Samaritan woman, putting away her feeling of humiliation and bitterness towards the Judeans/Jews, posed her question in the form of a statement. What she received from Jesus, she definitely did not expect to hear from a Judean:

> *"Jesus declared, 'Believe me, woman, a time is coming when you will worship the Father neither on this mountain nor in Jerusalem. You Samaritans worship what you do not know; we worship what we do know, for salvation is from 'the Jews'. Yet a time is coming and has now come when the true worshipers will worship the Father in spirit and truth, for they are the kind of worshipers the Father seeks. God is spirit, and his worshipers must worship in spirit and in truth'".*

She must have been stunned by his statement. Jesus challenged the main point of the Judean-Samaritan divide – the Mt. Gerizim vs. Mt. Zion controversy – arguing that the time had come for another type of worship altogether. In English, we can say "we will worship *on* that mountain," but when we are talking about the city we say "we will worship *in* that city". This is also the case in Greek, but in Hebrew, in which no doubt this conversation took place, Jesus would literally have said: "Believe me, woman, a time is coming when you will worship the Father neither "in" this mountain *nor* "in" Jerusalem. Yet a time is coming and has now come when the true worshipers will worship the Father "in" spirit and truth.

The third "in" therefore suggests that the enigmatic phrase: "to worship God in Spirit and in Truth", should be understood in the context of three mountains, not two (Mt. Gerizim, Mt. Zion and the Mt. [of] Spirit and Truth). Jesus is saying to the Samaritan woman that she must look up to another mountain. The choice was not between Jerusalem and Shechem (Mt. Zion and Mt. Gerizim). The choice was between Mt. Gerizim and the Mountain [of] Spirit and Truth.

The stunning phraseology that Jesus used in his next statement: "You Samaritans worship what you do not know; we worship what we do know, for salvation is from 'the Jews'" (4:22), spells the end of the idea that this Gospel is Samaritan, as some scholars (noting in-depth Samaritan interest) have erroneously concluded. Jesus could not have made this point any clearer. When it came to the Judeo-Samaritan conflict, he was with the Judeans. "We (Judeans) know" and "you Samaritans do not know" what we worship. The most striking statement in the entire Gospel, however, given

its overabundance of anti-Judean rhetoric, is –
"Salvation is from 'the Jews'/Judeans."

What could Jesus possibly mean here? Certainly, it
cannot be seriously entertained that he was saying that
the sub-group that sought his death and, at least in its
leadership, decisively rejected him, was going to lead
all Israel to salvation. What then did he mean?

The preliminary question to ask is whether, upon
hearing this statement of Jesus, the Samaritan woman,
who we now realize was well versed in Torah and
Torah-observance, would hold her peace. What must
Jesus appeal to in order for the Samaritan woman to
be convinced? The answer is - the shared Torah
tradition between Judeans and Samaritans. There is
one text in the Torah that fits this perfectly.

In Genesis 49:8-10, a passage that is in both the
Judean and Samaritan versions of the Torah, we read:

> "Judah, your brothers will praise you; your hand
> will be on the neck of your enemies; your father's
> sons will bow down to you. The scepter will not
> depart from Judah, nor the ruler's staff from
> between his feet, until he to whom it belongs shall
> come and the obedience of the nations shall be
> his".

Domination of enemies and guarantee of security were
the essential elements of the ancient concept of
salvation. No one at that time had thought of salvation
in Western individualistic terms. Judah would lead and
rule all others until *someone comes*, whom even the

nations will joyfully serve. When Jesus referred to this text, the Samaritan woman silently agreed.

You will recall that Jesus had already stated that the center of earthly worship was to be relocated from physical Jerusalem to the heavenly Jerusalem, concentrated in Himself when he spoke to Nathanael (1:50-51). He had invoked the great Torah story of Jacob's dream of the angels of God ascending and descending on the Holy Land of Israel where he was sleeping. (Gen. 18:12) He said to Nathanael that very soon the angels would be ascending and descending, not on Bethel (in Hebrew – House of God), which Samaritans identified as Mt. Gerizim, but upon the ultimate House of God – Jesus himself (Jn. 1:14; Jn. 2:21).

The official Samaritan religion, at least as far as we know from much later sources, did not include any prophetic writings, which means the Samaritan woman would have only Torah to rely upon in her definition of a Messiah-like figure. "The woman said, 'I know that *Messiah* (called Christ) is coming. When he comes, he will explain/teach everything to us'". We read in Deuteronomy 18:18-19, which is perfectly consistent with what the woman said: "I will raise up for them a prophet like you from among their brothers; I will put my words in his mouth, and he will tell them everything I command him. If anyone does not listen to my words that the prophet speaks in my name, I myself will call him to account".

Though a later Samaritan text speaks of a Messiah-*like* figure (Taheb, *Marqah Memar* 4:7, 12), the Samaritans of Jesus' time only expected a great teacher-prophet.

The "Messiah" as King and Priest was a Jewish Israelite, and not a Samaritan Israelite concept, as far as we know. For that reason, the reply of the

Samaritan woman shows this was not an imaginary or symbolic conversation ("he will *explain* everything to us"). In view of this, it seems that now the woman graciously used distinctly Jewish terminology to relate to Jesus – the Jew. Just as Jesus was choosing to climb the wall of taboos, so now was the Samaritan woman.

> *[25]The woman said, "I know that Messiah" (called Christ) "is coming. When he comes, he will explain everything to us". [26]Then Jesus declared, 'I who speak to you am he'.*

The story quickly switches to the return of the disciples, their reaction and commentary-like interaction with Jesus. This interchange is sandwiched between the encounters with the Samaritan woman and the men of her village. The disciples were surprised at seeing him conversing with the Samaritan woman, but no one challenged him about the inappropriateness of such an encounter.

I must take a brief aside from this conversation to explain something about a special feature of this Gospel. I believe the Gospel of John was initially written for a particular audience consisting of a variety of intra-Israelite groups, one of the main ones being the Samaritan Israelites. To them, unlike for us today, the word Ἰουδαῖοι (pronounced *Ioudaioi* and translated as "Jews") did not mean "the People of Israel," i.e. "the Jewish people" as we call them today. For these people, the people I propose are one of the main audiences for the Gospel of John, the *Ioudaioi*, meant something different.

48

Jerusalem, the heart of Judea as opposed to Samaria was the seat of power that exercised control and governing dominance over those who called themselves Jews. Not for everyone, but for John's audience of marginalized intra-Israelite groups the members of the Jerusalem-led system became *the Ioudaioi*. So when the audience for John's Gospel heard these anti-*Ioudaioi* statements (like John 7:1-2), whom did they think the author/s had in mind? This is the key question. Did they think of average Jews or the elites who ruled Jerusalem and those who identified with them?

To Samaritan Israelites, whatever else the *Ioudaioi* may have been, they were certainly Judeans - members of the former Southern Kingdom of Israel who had adopted a wide variety of innovations that were contrary to the Torah as Samaritans understood it. Judging from this Gospel, the original audience understood that, as well as simply being Judeans, the *Ioudaioi* were: i) Judean authorities, and ii) affiliated members of this authority structure living outside of Judea. These affiliates were located both in the territories of the former Northern Kingdom of Israel (Galilee) and in the large Israelite diaspora outside the Land of Israel, both in the Roman Empire and beyond. In this way, the Gospel of John, like the other Gospels, portrayed Jesus' antagonists as representatives of sub-groups within Israel, and not the people of Israel as a whole. In other words, *Ioudaioi* ("the Jews" in most translations) in this Gospel are not "the Jewish People" in the modern sense of the word.

The translation of *Ioudaioi* always and only as "Jews" sends the reader of John's Gospel in the opposite direction from what the author intended. While the translation of this word simply as "Judeans," is a more accurate choice than "Jews," it is still not fully adequate - for three reasons that come to mind:

The English word *Jews* evokes, in the minds of modern peoples, the idea of Jewish religion (i.e. Jews are people who profess a religion called Judaism) and therefore cannot be used *indiscriminately* to translate the term *Ioudaioi*, since, in the first century, there was no separate category for religion (*Judaism*, when it was used, meant something much more all-encompassing than what it means to us today). In a sense, it was only when non-Israelite Christ-followers, in an attempt to self-establish and self-define, created the category called *Christianity*, that the category called *Judaism*, as we know it today, was also born. Since then most Christian theologians and most Jewish theologians after them project our modern definition of Judaism back into the New Testament.

On the other hand, the English word *Judean* evokes in the minds of modern people, oftentimes, an almost exclusively geographical definition (a *Judean* is a person who lives in Judea or used to live in Judea) and hence cannot be used *indiscriminately* either, since today it does not imply everything it intended to imply in late antiquity.

The word *Judean*, without clarification and nuance, does not account for the complex relationship of the outside-of-Judea affiliates with the Jerusalem authorities either. Because of the lack of a perfect word to describe what was meant by *Ioudaioi* in the Gospel of John, I suggest that the word is best left untranslated.

Second, the Gospel of John was not composed as a pro-Samaritan or a Samaritan document. It was neither authored by Samaritan followers of Jesus nor sought to portray the Samaritans as more faithful to Torah than Judeans. It is a Judean-Israelite document that was originally composed to reach Samaritan and other Israelites with the gospel.

Why do I call this Israelite document *Judean*? Because it is especially in this Gospel that Jesus is shown as belonging to the *Ioudaioi*. As was already mentioned above, Jesus identified on a number of occasions with the *Ioudaioi (Judeans/Jews)*. In John 1:11b the *Ioudaioi* are "his own." In John 4:9 Jesus is called *Ioudaios (Judean/Jew)*. In John 4:22 Jesus and his disciples affirm that salvation is from the *Ioudaioi*, and in John 19:40 Jesus was buried according to the burial customs of the *Ioudaioi*.

On the other hand, if this Gospel is not Samaritan, but Judean in origin (ideologically and not necessarily geographically), what then explains such an acute interest in Samaritan Israelites?

This Gospel was authored by a certain kind of Judean (or more accurately a group of Judeans). He/they expected the coming redemption of Israel to include the return of the Samaritan Israelites (Jn. 4:35), as well as all the Children of Israel, dispersed among foreign lands. (Jn. 10:16; 11:52) The Gospel was probably written in the aftermath of the apostolic mission to the Samaritan lands (Acts 8) and probably provided an alternative to the Gospel of Matthew's anti-Samaritan views.

The Gospel of Matthew and the Gospel of John display similar tensions to those in the Books of Kings and Chronicles in the Hebrew Bible/Old Testament. The Books of Kings represent a Judean-centered narrative, telling, in many ways, a story similar to that of the Chronicles. One of the main differences was that the Books of Chronicles, though likely also of Judean authorship, had an "All Israel" perspective at the center. (1 Chron. 9:1; 11:1, 4, 10; 12:38; 13:5, 6, 8; 14:8; 2 Chron. 1:2; 7:6, 8; 9:30; 10:1, 3, 16) They refused to define Israel only as the Southern Israelites, later termed *Judeans*.

Similarly, it seems that the Gospel of John (and most probably the Gospel of Luke) was the alternative to the Gospel of Matthew's Judean anti-Samaritan views. (Matt. 10:5) John's Gospel, like the Books of Chronicles, called for all Israel to be united under the leadership of God's anointed king. In John's case, he envisioned Jesus as the King who came to unite representatives/descendants of both Southern and Northern tribes wherever they may be. (John 10:16) Just like the Gospel of Luke, this Gospel declared its firm belief in the coming "Messianic Reunification" that was promised by the prophets of old.

Third, the Gospel of John, like the three other Gospels, is technically an anonymous document. Later Christian tradition branded all four Gospels to associate with one of the great figures of the early Jesus movement. What can be said, however, is that the Gospel of John was authored by one for whom the Book of Ezekiel was particularly important. There is an overwhelming number of connections between these two Israelite works. This is, of course, not to say that Ezekiel is the only background for this Gospel; certainly, other books, like the Book of Daniel, are also extremely important. The use of Daniel in John's Gospel, however, is almost always connected with the night visions of Daniel (Dan. 7:13-14); while the Book of Ezekiel is alluded to throughout the Gospel by a multiplicity of themes.

One of these key themes in Ezekiel, just as I think in John, is the reunification of Southern and Northern Israel under the leadership of God's anointed King. (Ezek. 37:16; John 10:16) Some other compelling examples include: the Good Shepherd of Israel coming in judgment against the evil shepherds who neglect and exploit the sheep under their care (Ezek. 34:1-31; Jn. 10:11); the vision of the Temple bursting open with streams of running water which reach to the Dead Sea and beyond with revitalizing power (Ezek. 47:1-12; Jn. 7:38); and the Son of Man commanding God's Spirit to come and resurrect the people of Israel. (Ezek. 37:9-10; Jn. 16:7)

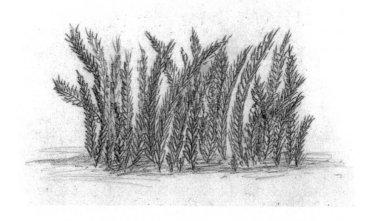

Forth, half of the Gospel (chapters 1-12) seems to cover three years of Jesus' ministry, judging from the three Passovers, while the second half (chapters 13-21) is concentrated on his Passion alone - roughly one day, culminating in his death and subsequent resurrection. I conclude, therefore, that the last half of the work is very important to the author's argument, with the chapters 1-12 serving as a disproportionate introduction to the Gospel's crescendo.

In this section, Jesus is on trial before the Judean and the Roman authorities. Yet, from the perspective of its author, the entire Gospel shows that it is the Judean authorities who are on trial. It is Jesus who has come as the covenant prosecutor to press charges against the evil shepherds of Israel. Not the other way around, as it may seem. While Jesus stands before his accusers and before Pilate, it is Jesus who has full power and authority. (Jn. 10:18; 19:11) From the very beginning, Jesus methodically worked his way to his goal, orchestrating and carefully controlling all the events surrounding his life (Jn. 11:6; 11:17; 12:14-15) and his Passion. (Jn. 19:28) The idea of a court motif is everywhere present in John.

Throughout the Gospel, we see many witnesses. Everyone and everything seems to be testifying in favor of Jesus (John 1:7; 4:39; 5:32; 19:35; 21:24); mounting evidence, piece-by-piece, is methodically presented. The inadequacy of the current *Ioudaioi* as leaders of God's people Israel is increasingly emphasized. (Jn. 3:9-10; 6:31-32; 8:21-22) Ultimately, their opposition to God's Anointed One (Jesus) is exemplified by their attempt to preserve Judea's Temple worship and therefore to prosper for themselves, their families and their sects, under the terms dictated by the Roman occupation. (Jn. 11:48) Such aims disqualify them to be the proper leaders of the Children of Israel.

Even though seven miraculous signs (Jn. 2:1-11; 4:46-54; 5:1-18; 6:5-14; 6:16-24; 9:1-7; 11:1-45) together testify to Jesus' power and divine authority, in the end, the ultimate justification of Jesus' person, words and deeds over against the formal rulers of Israel, is set forth – the resurrection of the Son of God as manifested by the empty tomb and three post-resurrection appearances. (Jn. 20-21)

Fifth, John's Gospel has a very interesting use of the word *world* (kosmos) throughout its narrative and it does not seem to be what we traditionally understand it to mean. The basic working definition of the term, "the world," in this Gospel seems to be *the order that opposes Israel's God.* (Jn. 7:7; 9:39; 12:31; 15:18-19) This opposing order is nevertheless an object of his redemptive love, attention, and restoration, (Jn. 1:29; 3:16; 6:33; 14:31; 17:23) because it was once created by God through his everlasting Word. (Jn. 1:1, 10) The primary identity of the *world* in this intra-Israelite Gospel is, not surprisingly – the current *Ioudaioi* and their leadership structure, especially. (Jn. 7:4-7; 8:23; 9:39; 14:17-31; 18:20)

This Gospel was written from one of the first century Judean perspectives, where Jesus' identity and the mission were intimately tied up with the *Ioudaioi,* as a sub-group within the nation of Israel. This affiliation of Jesus with the *Ioudaioi* was paramount for John's Gospel. Although Jesus is rejected by his own group, it belonged to him (Jn. 1:11; 4:22; 19:40). References like these, among many others, in my mind explain the pro-*Ioudaioi* statements in the Gospel.

At the same time, I propose that this first-century Judean perspective included a vision for the restoration of the Northern (Samaritan and Galilean) Israelites, as well as those residing in the Judean and Samaritan diaspora centers outside of the Land. To the author of this Gospel, Jesus was nothing less than the King of Israel in its entirety.

It is especially for those Israelites (whether Samaritan, Galilean or residing in diaspora) that this Gospel was first written. This, in my mind, accounts for the anti-*Ioudaioi* statements we find in this Israelite Gospel. The anti-*Ioudaioi* statements would not be understood by these late first century Israelites (or Gentile God-fearers for that matter) as criticizing Israel as a whole. In spite of what Christian and Jewish theologians after them have assumed about John's Gospel, it was not originally meant to be read by everyone. It may even be said that the composition of John's Gospel constituted a significant lack of foresight on behalf of its (human) author. Had the author imagined (and the fact that he also didn't give us insight into the first century Jesus movement) that, just few centuries later, it would be primarily non-Israelites who would read and interpret his magnificent Gospel, being removed culturally and socio-religiously from its original setting, he might have been much more careful with the use of his terminology.

So, how can the Gospel of John seem/be pro-Jewish and anti-Jewish all at the same time? Because: 1) It is a Judean Gospel at its core, and 2) It was originally written to Israelites who understood that *Ioudaioi* were but a sub-group within Israel and not "the Jewish People" as a whole.

Although the idea that John's Gospel was at first meant only for Israelites may be threatening to some people, there is absolutely nothing to fear. Most of the books in the Bible had a specific audience, even if most of the time we can only guess who that audience really was. The message of these sacred texts, after being properly understood, can and must legitimately be applied to other contexts as well, and this, my friends, includes everyone who would be willing to hear the message of this Gospel. Now let's return to the conversation at the well.

> *27 Just then his disciples returned and were surprised to find him talking with a woman. But no one asked, "What do you want?" or "Why are you talking with her?" 28 Then, leaving her water jar, the woman went back to the town and said to the people, 29 "Come, see a man who told me everything I ever did. Could this be the Christ?" 30 They came out of the town and made their way toward him. 31 Meanwhile his disciples urged him, "Rabbi, eat something". 32 But he said to them, "I have food to eat that you know nothing about". 33 Then his disciples said to each other, "Could someone have brought him food?" 34 "My food," said Jesus, "is to do the will of him who sent me and to finish his work" (John 4:27-34).*

While it is possible that the disciples were surprised that he was alone in conversation with a woman, the general context of the story seems to indicate that their response had more to do with him conversing with a woman who was a Samaritan. It is interesting that none of the disciples could even imagine that Jesus would partake of the food from the nearby Samaritan village (once again due to the issues of variant purity requirements among Samaritans and Judeans). Instead, they wondered if some other disciples had gone to bring him food. (The Gospel does not say that all the disciples went to buy food in the nearby town). Later on, Jesus would show his disciples that he had no problem with the purity laws the Samaritans followed. Later in the story, we see that he lodged with them for two days (Jn. 4:40). But before that happened, Jesus had a lot to explain.

The laws of purity, the notions of clean vs. unclean, the thinking that one food is acceptable and another is unacceptable simply because it comes from outsiders is yet another concept modern readers of the gospels find confusing. In fact, traditional Christain interpretations of many New Testament passages make this topic even more puzzling. From a Christian perspective, purity laws are deemed useless. As a result they are rarely even studied and that is why many New Testament teachings where they are mentioned are often completely misunderstood.

For example, in Mark 7 we read about a sharp debate between Judean Pharisees and Jesus over the fact that his Galilean disciples did not follow an important Pharisaic innovation introduced long ago. This innovation had to do with the perceived need to ensure that prior to consuming clean/fit and properly prepared food, a person must also wash hands, in order not to make something that is already holy, common by accident. By the time the conflict recounted in Mark 7 occurred, this Pharisaic innovation had already become "a tradition of the elders" and was treated as such, with great respect by most Judeans (vs. 1-4).

Quoting Isaiah, Jesus accuses the Pharisees of neglecting the commandments of Torah, holding instead to the tradition of man (vs. 8). Addressing the crowd, Jesus states: "There is nothing outside the man which can defile him if it goes into him, but the things which proceed out of the man are what defile the man" (vs. 15). This was but a summary of regulations governing bodily discharges as spelled out in Leviticus 15. These bodily discharges come out of the body and do not enter it. According to Jesus, a much deeper spiritual reality is concealed here – namely, that all evil comes out into the world from the human heart (meaning inside out not the other way around) (vs.20-23).

Some rightly seeking to reclaim the intensely Jewish character of Mark's gospel has mistakenly suggested that vs. 19 (*Thus He* declared all foods clean) is an editorial addition to the original text, made by Gentile Christians disinterested in Jewish issues. I suggest, however, that this line is in fact, an integral part of Mark's very Jewish argument! The law of bodily discharge is a case in point. Defending Torah against the Pharisees, Jesus upholds a long-standing Galilean Jewish tradition, declaring that foods cannot make an Israelite unclean, because in Torah it works the other way around!

I realize that my take on this familiar passage may be the opposite of what you have been taught. I merely propose for you to read these passages from the vantage point of spiritual dialogue within the Jewish culture and not a discussion of one religious group with another. And I can imagine that a few more verses come up in your remembrance that make you skeptical of my commentary. How can Mark's Gospel affirm the purity laws? Because there are so many other places, especially in Paul's letters that seem to suggest the opposite. But do they? Sometime later Paul wrote to Timothy:

> "…*some will fall away from the faith…forbidding marriage, abstaining from foods which God has created to be gratefully shared in by those who believe and know the truth. For everything created by God is good, and nothing is to be rejected if it is received with gratitude, for it is sanctified by*

means of the word of God and prayer" (1 Tim. 4:1-4).

The traditional interpretation is that Paul was instructing Timothy to oppose the Torah's division of things into "clean" and "unclean". It assumes that Torah's unclean foods were meant in the above text. However, such a reading is problematic for the two following reasons:

First, such an interpretation ignores the fact that "the entire creation is good because God declared it so" is a universally upheld Jewish idea (Gen.1:25). Second, just because God's creation is good, it does not follow that all of it can be used for food by Israelites (Lev. 11:13). In fact, Paul specifically states that anything can be eaten only if two specific conditions are met: God has sanctified it by His Word, and the worshiper has sanctified it by his/her prayer (1 Tim. 4:4).

God's Word that Paul and Timothy read does not sanctify what it expressly forbids. Paul instructed Timothy to remember, especially after his circumcision, that he must honor the God of Israel in every detail of his life as a Christ-following Jew, including the way he ate. Did Paul tell Jewish Timothy to eat unclean? No, in fact, he told him the exact opposite!

I am persuaded that Jesus and other Jews described on the pages of the New Testament maintained purity laws and lived according to the Jewish lifestyle. This may be a new revelation for you. Traditional Christian teaching often maintains that Timothy and Paul, Peter and John have all abandoned the old ways. Yet that is not what read on the pages New Testament.

While admonishing Peter to live in accordance with the Gospel, Paul stated that he (Peter) while being a Judean, "lived" as a member of the nations and not (uniquely) as a Judean (Gal.2:14). Most people today wrongly conclude that Paul was describing Peter's non-Jewish lifestyle, which is why Paul's argument seems to make no sense. Yet the very basis of the conflict between the two apostles suggests otherwise. After all, the conflict was over fellowship with Gentiles who did not go through proselyte conversion.

These Gentiles worshiped Israel's God in Christ but did not completely obligate themselves to full Torah observance. They, therefore, remained members of the nations of the world. (Remember that the basic problem with Gentiles was not their genetic identity, but their non-Jewish lifestyle, which would have put them out of the possibility of fellowship with the rest of the Jewish people). This background, together with Peter's apostolic commissioning to primarily minister to Judeans, renders our modern de-Judaized interpretation (of "you live as a Gentile") nothing short of absurd.

Paul also told Peter that: "We who are 'Jews' by birth and not Gentile 'sinners' know that a man is not justified by works of the Torah" (Gal. 2:15-16a). The Apostle Paul did not refer to Peter's lifestyle, but rather to his experience in Christ! This was very much in line with what Peter witnessed himself when Israel's God poured out His Spirit on Gentile God-fearers (Acts 10). That is without becoming proselyte converts (meaning without becoming fully committed to the entire Torah) the Gentile God-fearers became recipients of the Holy Spirit of Israel's God!

In other words, "live as a Gentile" did not mean that Peter abandoned his Jewish lifestyle, but that he was now alive in Christ in exactly the same way as Gentiles were – by grace through faith, and not because of obedience to the Torah (Eph.2:1-22). So, did Peter, and for that matter, Paul, "live" as Gentiles? Absolutely! They were made alive in Christ in the same way as Gentiles were (Gal. 2:15-16)!

This may not be how you have always understood this passage, but consider my perspective and allow a possibility that much of what we embrace as solid interpretations are in fact quite subjective, especially when we talk about things we do not even believe or practice.

I am sharing these reflections on New Testament passages because they are tied to the rejection of purity laws, to the notions of clean vs. unclean which are often accompanied by restricting table fellowship. In John Jesus was willing to accept not only drink from the Samaritan woman but food as well. In fact, he and his disciples did just that. Remember, the Samaritans were Israelites and for the most part, obeyed the same rules of Torah. There was ideological and political reason to reject their food and friendship, but there is no reason to think their food would be radically different from the food of other Israelites.

Leaving behind her jar, the woman rushed to town to tell her people about Jesus, posing an important question to them: "Could this be the one whom Israel has been waiting for so long?" Speaking as he did in the context of the encounter, Jesus pointed out to his disciples that what he was doing was purely and simply God's will. Doing the will of his Father gave him his divine life energy. This divine energy enabled him to continue his work. We continue reading:

> [35] *"Do you not say, 'Four months more and then the harvest?' I tell you, open your eyes and look at the fields! They are ripe for harvest.* [36]*Even now the reaper draws his wages; even now he harvests the crop for eternal life, so that the sower and the reaper may be glad together.* [37]*Thus the saying 'One sows and another reaps' is true.* [38]*I sent you to reap what you have not worked for. Others have done the hard work, and you have reaped the benefits of their labour".*

In these verses, Jesus challenged his disciples to consider the crop that was ready for harvest. It is almost certain that Jesus' disciples thought the spiritual harvest pertained to the Jerusalem-affiliated Israelites alone. Jesus challenged them to look outside their box, to the neighboring heretical and adversarial community, for the harvest – a harvest field they had not considered until this encounter. The significance of Jesus' commentary on the encounter was not to highlight the importance of evangelism in general, but rather to bring attention to fields that were previously unseen, or thought of as unsuitable for the harvest.

He, the King of Israel, will unite the North and the South as part of his restoration program for Israel. We read in Amos 9:11-15:

> *"'In that day I will raise up the booth of David that is fallen and repair its breaches, and raise up its ruins and rebuild it as in the days of old, that they may possess the remnant of Edom and all the nations who are called by my name', declares the Lord who does this. 'Behold, the days are coming', declares the lord, 'when the plowman shall overtake the reaper and the trader of grapes him who sows the seed; the mountains shall drip sweet wine, and all the hills shall flow with it. I will restore the fortunes of my people Israel, and they shall rebuild the ruined cities and inhabit them; they shall plant vineyards and drink their wine, and they shall make gardens and eat their fruit. I will plant them on their land, and they shall never again be uprooted out of the land that I have given them', says the Lord your God."*

In the book of Acts, we read of a significant move of God's Spirit among Samaritans and the openness that the Judean Jesus-following communities had for these new-found brothers and sisters in the faith. (Acts 8) We might also recall Jesus' post-resurrection instructions to the disciples not to leave Jerusalem. He told them "...you shall be my witnesses both in Jerusalem, and in all Judea AND SAMARIA, and even to the remotest part of the earth" (Acts 1:8).

It has been traditionally assumed that Samaria was simply a geographical half-way point between Jewish Judea and the Gentile ends of the earth. As I will argue later, this was certainly not the case. We read that the apostles preached the Gospel in the Samaritan villages, actually implementing Jesus' directive: "... they started back to Jerusalem and were preaching the gospel TO MANY VILLAGES OF THE SAMARITANS" (Acts 8:25). We are told, "the apostles in Jerusalem heard that Samaria had accepted the word of God". That is to say, in comparison to many others, the Samarian lands were very receptive to the gospel (Acts 8:9-14).

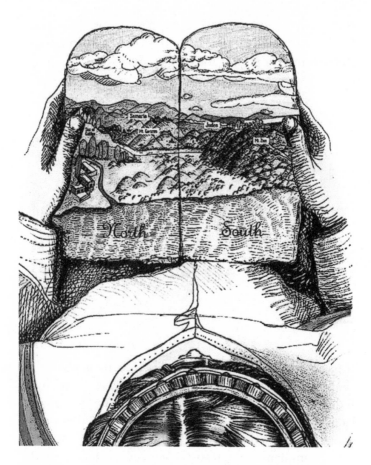

The Samaritan Israelites, unlike today, constituted a sizable number of people who claimed to have been a remnant of the Northern tribes of Israel. Some recent studies in reputable secular scientific journals on DNA research show that there is a genetic link between modern Samaritans and Israelite priests of old. It is very difficult to speak in precise numbers, but scholars who focus their research on Samaritans suggest that their first-century population was roughly equal (or almost equal) to the size of the Judean Israelites, both in the Land and in Diaspora.

The other Gospels, especially Matthew, were too Judea-centered, and even anti-Samaritan, to be suitable for use among Samaritan Israelites. We read in Matt. 10:5-6: "These twelve Jesus sent out after instructing them: 'Do not go in the way of the Gentiles, and do not enter any city of the Samaritans; but rather go to the lost sheep of the house of Israel'". Matthew's Jesus couples Gentiles with Samaritans and emphasizes the command (at least at this stage of the ministry) not to go to Samaritan villages. In his great commission (Matt. 28:19-20), Matthew again displays this view by having Jesus command his Jewish Israelite disciples to simply make disciples of all nations, without paying special attention to the Samaritan Israelites.

While Jesus was no doubt conversing with his followers about the suitability of teaching the Samaritans God's ways, he heard voices from the crowd approaching him from a distance. The faithful witness of this Gospel describes it like this:

> *"Many of the Samaritans from that town believed in him because of the woman's testimony, 'He told me everything I ever did'. So when the Samaritans came to him, they urged him to stay with them, and he stayed two days. And because of his words many more became believers. They said to the woman, 'We no longer believe just because of*

*what you said; now we have heard for
ourselves, and we know that this man really is
the Saviour of the world"' (verses 39-42).*

Interpreting the Bible is a difficult task. We bring our
past, our preconceived notions, our already formed
theology, our cultural blind spots, our social standing,
our gender, our political views, and many other
influences to our interpretation of the Bible. In short,
all that we are in some way determines how we
interpret everything. This does not imply that the
meaning of the text is dependent on its reader. The
meaning remains constant. But the reading of the text
does differ and is dependent on many factors
surrounding the interpretive process. In other words,
how a reader or listener understands the text can differ
greatly from person to person.

One of the biggest handicaps in the enterprise of Bible
interpretation has been an inability to recognize and
admit that a particular interpretation may have a weak
spot. The weak spot is usually determined by personal
preferences and heartfelt desires to prove a particular
theory, regardless of the cost. I consider that having an
awareness of our own blind spots and being honestly
willing to admit problems with our interpretations
when they exist, is more important than the
intellectual brilliance with which we argue our
position.

One opportunity to exercise an honest approach is
when commentators recognize that there is something
in their interpretation that does not seem to fit with

70

the text and they do not quite know how to explain it. What I feel can be legitimately suggested as a challenge to our reading of the story of the Samaritan woman, are the words the Gospel author places on her lips when she tells her fellow villagers about her encounter with Jesus. She says: "He told me everything *I ever did*". It would have matched the traditional interpretation perfectly if her words had been: "He told me everything that happened to me" or better yet "was done to me".

I think, once again, we are so preconditioned to think in Christian terms ("we are all fallen people, but especially the Samaritan woman" kind of approach) that we are unable to read this sentence positively. In other words, *everything I ever did*, maybe just that – a simple statement that the entire life of the woman was known to Jesus (not necessarily a life of sexual immorality).

This phrase is probably a statement of amazement that here is an outsider, someone who does not really know me, yet he knows very private things about me. He knows my pain, my sorrow of loss (and/or divorce) of multiple husbands, the struggle of getting married again. How can this Judean know this and understand the pain and the stigma that I have to live with? Yet he offers me living water and life...

In other words, this verse should be understood differently – "he knows everything about me". Indeed, she would hardly have gone bragging to the townspeople that "this stranger told me all the sinful acts I have done in my life." When we think of it, that would hardly have sent them running to meet him, but rather sent them running in the other direction! But I realize that getting over preconceived notions and interpretive preconditioning is not easy. It was Krister Stendahl who said, "Our vision is often more abstracted by what we think we know than by our lack of knowledge".

> [43] *After two days he departed for Galilee* [44]*for Jesus himself had testified that a prophet has no honor in his own hometown.* [45]*So when he came to Galilee, the Galileans welcomed him, having seen all that he had done in Jerusalem at the feast. For they too had gone to the feast.* [46] *So he came again to Cana in Galilee, where he had made the water wine. And at Capernaum there was an official whose son was ill.* [47] *When this man heard that Jesus had come from Judea to Galilee, he went to him and asked him to come down and heal his son, for he was at the point of death.* [48] *So Jesus said to him, "Unless you see signs and wonders you will not believe".* [49] *The official said to him, "Sir, come down before my child dies".* [50] *Jesus said to him, "Go; your son will live". The man believed the word that Jesus spoke to him and went on his way.* [51] *As he was going down, his servants met him and told him that his son was recovering.* [52] *So he asked them the hour when he began to get better, and they said to him, "Yesterday at the*

seventh hour the fever left him". [53] The father
knew that was the hour when Jesus had said
to him, "Your son will live". And he himself
believed, and all his household. [54] This was
now the second sign that Jesus did when he
had come from Judea to Galilee.

As the reporting of the events connected with Jesus'
stopover in Samaritan Shechem finishes, we come to
John 4:43-45. Here we see that Jesus does not return
to Judea but continues his journey to Galilee.

In addition to the absence of the incident with the
Samaritan woman from the Synoptics, there is another
significant feature in which the Synoptics and John
part company. John states the reason Jesus did not
return to Judea but went on to Galilee, was because
"Jesus himself had testified that a prophet has no
honor in his own homeland". (Literally: "fatherland"
in the sense of "motherland" in the English language)
(4:44). What is, of course, striking here is that John
names Judea as Jesus' homeland, his fatherland, and
not Galilee as do the Synoptics (Mt 13:54-57, Mk. 6:1-
4, Lk. 4:23-24).

It is likely that the Synoptics treat Galilee, the place of
Jesus' upbringing, as his fatherland. For John,
however, Jesus is Judean because of his birth in
Bethlehem of Judea. To John, Jesus lived in Galilee
because of God's mission and not because of his
Galilean identity. To John, he was a Judean.

Together with this alternative reading of Jesus' identity, John paints a picture for his readers of Jesus' rejection and acceptance, which is also very different from the picture in the Synoptics. Galilee and Samaria were very responsive to Jesus. People there welcomed him with very few exceptions; while everything he did in his homeland of Judea seemed to meet significant opposition.

There a paradox here, a tension. In Judea (Jesus' motherland in John) Jesus faced persecution. He was born there and his Father's house, the Temple of Israel's God, was in Jerusalem (not in Galilee and not in Samaria), but it is from there that the real opposition to his ministry came. It is not that unbelief was found only in Judea after all some Galilean Jewish disciples would leave Jesus after his statements about his body and blood (Jn. 6:66). But all in all, it cannot be denied that Samaria and Galilee were far more receptive to Jesus than was Judea. I suggest once again, therefore, that we should understand John 1:11 within this context of: "He came to his own, and his own people did not receive him".

The image of the Samaritan Woman at the well should be reconsidered. Not just her looks, but who she really was and that entire conversation. This rethinking is a good beginning and we may only have scratched the surface. How many more things about ancient life in Judea and Samaria we truly do not understand? How often do we read these stories and allow our own culture to blind us from being able to see the reality?

We may never know. But one sure step we can take to correct this is to make a permanent attitude adjustment and realize how the things we think we know can make it hard for us to discover the truth. They get in our way. So let us continue rereading the Bible, keeping our modern thinking in check, and let us continue asking good questions!

Dear reader, if you enjoyed this book and would like to see more books like this one, drop me a line and let me know dr.eli.israel@gmail.com.

Dr. Eli Lizorkin-Eyzenberg

Made in the USA
Coppell, TX
26 September 2021